BARRON'S
POCKET GUIDE TO
CORRECT
ENGLISH

BARRON'S POCKET GUIDE TO
CORRECT ENGLISH

Fourth Edition

Michael Temple

Fourth U.S. Edition (revised) 2004 by Barron's Educational Series, Inc.
Third U.S. Edition (revised) 1997 by Barron's Educational Series, Inc.
Second U.S. Edition (revised) 1990 by Barron's Educational Series, Inc.
First U.S. Edition 1982 by Barron's Educational Series, Inc.

© Michael Temple 1978

First published by John Murray (Publishers) Ltd. in 1978

All inquiries should be addressed to:
Barron's Educational Series, Inc.
250 Wireless Boulevard
Hauppauge, New York 11788
http://www.barronseduc.com

ISBN-13: 978-0-7641-2688-8
ISBN-10: 0-7641-2688-1

Library of Congress Catalog Card No. 2003045143

Library of Congress Cataloging-in-Publication Data
Temple, Michael
    A pocket guide to correct English / Michael Temple.—4th ed.
        p. cm.
    Includes index.
    ISBN 0-7641-2688-1
    1. English language—Grammar—Handbooks, manuals, etc.
    2. English language—Usage—Handbooks, manuals, etc. I. Title:
Correct English. II. Title.

PE1112.T43   2004
428.2—dc22   2003045143

PRINTED IN CHINA
9 8 7 6 5 4 3 2

Contents

Acknowledgments

I am grateful to my wife and colleagues for their valuable assistance and to my pupils, past and present, without whose errors I could not have written this book.

PART I

USING ENGLISH CORRECTLY

Chapter 1

Terms of English Usage and Grammar

Standard English usage is the name given to language generally spoken and written by literate, educated people. *Grammar*, on the other hand, is a set of rules that describes or defines the way words are used and sentences are constructed. In talking about usage and grammar, it helps to know the meaning of the eight so-called "parts of speech" (noun, pronoun, verb, adjective, adverb, conjunction, preposition, and interjection). It also helps to understand sentence structure; that is, how the elements of sentences— individual words, phrases, and clauses—work together to create meaning.

PARTS OF SPEECH

➤ A **noun** names a person, place, thing, or quality: *girl, camp, army, beauty, decision.* In a sentence, the words *the*, *a*, or *an* often indicate that the next word is a noun, as in *the girl, a camp, an army.* (*The* is called a *definite article*; *a* and *an* are called *indefinite articles*.)

A "proper" noun is the actual name of a person, place, or thing, such as *Lincoln, St. Louis, the Declaration of Independence*, and is always capitalized. All other nouns are called "common" nouns.

➤ A **pronoun** stands in place of a noun. For example:

> *he/she, him/her, me, it, them, you, anyone, who/whom, which, whose, that*

Pronouns are distinguished by *person*, *case*, and *number*.

> First person pronouns: *I, me*
> Second person pronouns: *you, your*
> Third person pronouns: *he, she, it, they, his, her*
>
> Nominative case pronouns: *I, we, you, he, she, it, they*
> Objective case pronouns: *me, him, her, it, us, you, them*
>
> Singular pronouns: *I, he, she, it, you,* etc.
> Plural pronouns: *we, you, they, them, their, our*

➤ A **verb** expresses an action (*talk, eat, bring*) or state of being (*is, am, are, will be*).

Verbs have several tenses that show when the action takes place. Among them:

> Present: talk, eat, bring
> Past: talked, ate, brought
> Present perfect: has talked, has eaten, has brought
> Past perfect: had talked, had eaten, had brought
> Future: will talk, will eat, will bring

Verbs also have forms related to number (singular/plural) and person (first/second/third). For example:

> First person singular: I *talk/talked*, I *eat/ate*, I *bring/brought*
> First person plural: we *talk/talked*, we *eat/ate*, we *bring/brought*

Second person plural: you *have talked*, you *have eaten*, you *had brought*
Third person singular: the man *talked*, Jennifer *will eat*, he/she *brought*
Third person plural: they *talk,* they *have eaten,* they *will bring*

Most verbs are formed according to a pattern. To change a verb from present to past tense, for example, add *-d* or *-ed*, as in *agree/agreed* and *shout/shouted*.

Verbs that do not follow this pattern are called *irregular*, and include *break/broke, ring/rang, slay/slew, put/put*, among hundreds of others. The most widely used irregular verb is the state-of-being verb *to be*. Forms of *to be* are shown below:

Infinitive: *to be*

	First Person	Second Person	Third Person
Present	*am, are*	*are*	*is, are*
Past	*was, were*	*were*	*was, were*
Present perfect	*have been*	*have been*	*have been*
Past perfect	*had been*	*had been*	*had been*
Future	*will be*	*will be*	*will be*

➤ An **adjective** describes, or modifies, a noun or pronoun. It can either stand in front of a noun, as in *black* cat, *perfect* work, the *quick, brown* fox, or it can refer back to the noun, as in the cat is *black*, the work was *perfect*, a fox is *quick* and *brown*.

To "modify" means to change or limit the noun described. For example, the noun *house* names a type of building. But any adjective, such as *big, blue, new, run-down, illuminated* describes, or modifies, the noun, thereby describing the house more specifically.

Comparisons are made by different forms of adjectives. The degree of comparison is indicated by the ending, usually *-er* or *-est*, or by the use of *more* or *most* (or *less* and *least*).

Adjective	Comparative	Superlative
hot	hotter	hottest
soon	sooner	soonest
good	better	best
beautiful	more beautiful	most beautiful
able	abler or more able	ablest or most able

➤ An **adverb** is a descriptive word that usually modifies a verb, telling how, where, when, or why an action is done, as in "Martha ran *quickly*." Here, the adverb *quickly* modifies the verb *ran*, telling how Martha ran.

An adverb can also modify an adjective or another adverb. In the phrase "very good," the adverb *very* modifies the adjective *good*. In the phrase "extremely well," the adverb *extremely* modifies *well*, another adverb.

Many adverbs are formed from adjectives to which the ending *-ly* has been added, as in *softly*, *freely*, and *ambitiously*.

➤ A **conjunction** joins or shows the relationship between words, phrases, or clauses, as in:

> ham *and* eggs; poor *but* honest; for better *or* worse; *although* he was injured, he played well

➤ A **preposition** introduces a phrase and is followed by a noun or pronoun. The phrase often tells you where, when, or how something happened, as in:

The vase is *on* the table.
They traveled *by* bicycle.
She climbed *up* the pole.
The horse ran *over* the hills.
Between you and me, I think she is lying.

Other prepositional phrases:

at the beach, *from* home, *toward* Toledo, *of* the people, *to* the mountain, *around* town, *through* the Internet

➤ An **interjection** is an exclamatory word or phrase. It can be taken out of a sentence without destroying the sense, as in:

Well, I'd like to go with you.
Oh dear, the sky is falling.
Yikes, here comes the bus.

SENTENCES

Words can be arranged in so many different ways that the definition of a sentence covering all possibilities has not yet been devised. Nevertheless, most complete sentences share certain characteristics. They consist of a subject and a verb. In addition, they often contain one or more phrases and clauses.

Subject

➤ The **subject** of a sentence is what is being talked about. It is a noun or pronoun, with or without modifiers.

Simple subject: *She* asked a question.
Compound subject: *She and her sick mother* entered the hospital.

Every sentence has a stated subject unless it gives a command or makes a request:

> Make mine without mustard.
> Please be ready at six.

In such sentences the noun or pronoun is omitted, but is understood to be "you."

Verb

➤ A sentence needs a **verb** to tell what the subject does or did, or to explain what the subject is or was.

> Lucy *ate* a pound of chocolate.
> Lucy *is* a chocolate freak.

Some words seem like verbs but are not verbs. These are called *verbals*, which may not be used as the main verb in a sentence. Verbals include the *infinitive* form of verbs (*to walk, to be considered, to have seen*) and *participles*.

A participle may act as an adjective, as in a *talking* doll.

A participle may also introduce an adjective phrase, as in

> *Talking* very loudly, they got on the bus.
> *Talked* about for months, the film quickly became a success.

Present participles end in *-ing*; past participles in *-ed* (usually). It helps to remember that no word ending in *-ing*, except one-syllable words like *sing* and *ring*, may serve as the verb of a sentence unless it is preceded by *is, are, was*, or some other *being* verb, as in *is arriving* and *are campaigning*.

When the subject is performing the action, the verb is said to be in the *active voice*, as in "Jack *built* the house." When the subject is suffering the action, the verb is said to be in the *passive voice*, as in "The house *was built* by Jack."

Predicate

➤ Everything in a sentence that is not the subject and its modifiers is called the **predicate**.

> Phil, the speed demon, works faster than George does on most jobs.

In this sentence, *Phil, the speed demon* is the subject; everything else is the predicate.

Phrases

Phrases are groups of related words that function in sentences as a noun, adjective, or adverb.

➤ *To write well* requires practice. (The italicized phrase acts as a noun. It is the subject of the verb *requires*.) Because the phrase is made up of the infinitive form of the verb, it is called an **infinitive phrase**.

Infinitive phrases may also serve as adjectives, as in: Oscar had the intent *to live in style* after retiring from the army. The italicized phrase modifies, or describes, Oscar's intent.

➤ Another phrase that functions as a noun is the **gerund phrase**. Running a mile is easy. *Running* is the gerund. *Mile* is its object. The phrase is the subject of the sentence.

➤ The boy *wearing the blue vest* placed second. The italicized phrase acts as an adjective, describing the noun boy. Hence the name **adjective phrase**.

➤ Put it *on the table*. The italicized phrase acts as an adverb, telling where the action is to be done, hence the name **adverbial phrase**. Because the phrase begins with the preposition *on*, the phrase is also called a **prepositional phrase**.

Clauses

A clause is a group of words containing a simple predicate. There are two basic types:

➤ **Main clause**—the "backbone" of the sentence. It often makes a simple sentence on its own (but see noun clauses below).

➤ **Subordinate clause**—this, like a phrase, acts as an adjective, adverb or noun, and depends upon the main clause. It cannot stand on its own.

> When you read a long sentence, *you should look for the main clause* that the subclauses depend on. (The main clause here is *italicized;* the other two clauses are subordinate.)

Types of Subordinate Clauses

➤ **Adjective clause**

> The man *who called yesterday* must have been a salesman. (The italicized words describe *the man.*)
>
> I found the book *(that) I had been searching for.* (Describes *book.*)

He was absent on the day *when it happened.*
(Describes *day.*)

➤ Adverb clause

There are various kinds:

– **Time:**

The crowd cheered *when the president appeared.*
(When?)

– **Place:**

He hid the gold *where no one would find it.*
(Where?)

– **Reason:**

She won *because she had more stamina.* (Why?)

– **Purpose:**

He worked hard *so that he would pass his exam.*
(With what intention?)

– **Result:**

They played so well *that they won the* blue ribbon.
(With what result?)

– **Condition:**

You will succeed *if you try hard.*
(On what condition?)

– **Concession:**

Although they played well, they still lost.
(In spite of what?)

– **Manner:**

They did *as they pleased.* (How?)

– **Degree** (or **comparison**):

She sings better *than I do.*
(To what extent? Compared with what?)

In all the above examples, the words *not* italicized
form the main clause.

➤ The **noun clause** may

– be the **subject** of the main verb:

Why he did it remains a mystery.

– be the **direct object** of the main verb:

I do not know *whether he will come.*

– be the **complement** of a verb of being:

This is *how we do it.*

– be **in apposition to** a previous noun or pronoun
(i.e., enlarging upon or restating it):

The idea *that he could be guilty* never crossed our
minds.

It never crossed our minds *that he was guilty.*

– follow a **preposition:**

The point of *what he said* eludes me.
He gave an account of *when it happened.*

TYPES OF SENTENCES

➤ A **simple sentence** contains a subject and verb, as in *Maria sings*. It can also contain various modifiers and a predicate, but it still consists of only one main clause, as in:

> *Maria, the girl in the green dress, sings like a canary.*

➤ A sentence containing two or more main clauses joined by a conjunction (and, but, or) is called a **compound sentence**.

> *Adam is growing up quickly and he looks more like his grandfather every day.*

➤ A sentence containing a main clause and one or more subordinate clauses is called a **complex sentence**.

> *Although Jim was late, he stopped at the deli on his way to work to buy a sandwich for lunch.*

Objects and Complements

In some sentences, nouns and pronouns function as objects and complements.

An *indirect object* is the person or thing to or for whom the action is done. A *direct object* is the person or thing affected by the action. (It often answers the question "Whom?" or "What?")

> Pass the ball to *her.*

As the recipient of the ball, *her* is the indirect object. As the thing affected by the action, *ball* is the direct object. In general, direct objects precede indirect objects in the word order of a sentence. If the indirect object is a pronoun, however, it may precede the direct object, as in:

> He gave *her* a book.

The *complement* completes the sense of verbs such as *be, become*, and *seem*:

> He is *an actor*. (*An actor* is the complement of the verb *is*.)

Transitive and Intransitive Verbs

Some verbs are called *transitive* verbs; others are *intransitive* verbs. A transitive verb takes an object, as in He woke his *sister*. *Sister* is the "object" of the verb *woke*.

> She boiled an *egg*. (*Egg* is the object of the verb *boiled*.)

An intransitive verb has no object, as in:

> She awoke. The water boiled.

Chapter 2

Solving Common Problems

In a language that is constantly changing there is always some conflict between current usage and established practice. Similarly, there are differences between what is permissible in popular speech and what is expected in formal writing. The following constructions refer to usage in formal writing.

AGREEMENT

A singular subject must have a singular verb, a plural subject a plural verb. Be sure to ask yourself whether the subject is singular or plural.

> *One* of the men *was* guilty.
> A *range* of goods *was* available.
> All along the coast *lie traces* of oil slick.

➤ **Indefinite pronouns**—i.e., *anyone, someone, no one, none, (n)either (n)or, everyone, each*—are singular and should take a singular verb and be followed by *he/she, him/her, his/her,* and NOT *they, them, their(s)*:

> No one knows *his* own future.
> Anyone can do it if *she* tries *her* best.
> Each stood with *his* right hand behind *his* back.

➤ **(N)either . . . (n)or.** If *both* the subjects are singular, the verb is also:

> Neither the woman nor the dog *was* in sight.

15

➤ If one subject is singular and one is plural, the verb agrees with the subject closer to the verb:

> Neither the books nor the map *is* on the table.
> Neither the map nor the books *are* on the table.

But verbs are not influenced by intervening phrases beginning with *in addition to, along with, as well as,* or other similar phrases.

> One of his paintings, in addition to several photos, *is* on display.
> Her parents, as well as Jennifer, *make* the decision.

➤ **This kind, this sort** (or **these kinds, these sorts**) but not *these kind, these sort.*

➤ **Collective nouns** which are groups of persons or things can take a singular verb when considered as a complete unit:

> The class *is* too large.

but a plural verb when considered as a number of separate persons or things:

> The class *were* quarrelling.

➤ **The verb in an adjective clause** must agree with the right noun or pronoun in the clause before it:

> She is one of the most famous writers who *have* ever lived.

Who relates back to *writers;* hence the plural *have.*

CASES

➤ **I, he, she, we, they,** and **who** are the subject pronouns.

> The man who will be king . . .

> > **WRONG:** John and me are brothers.
> > **RIGHT:** John and *I* are brothers.

> > **WRONG:** This is the man whom we all knew was guilty.
> > **RIGHT:** This is the man *who* (we all knew) was guilty.

The parentheses show that *who* is the subject of *was*.

> > **OR:** This is the man *whom* we all *knew to be* guilty.

➤ **Me, him, her, us, them,** and **whom** are the object pronouns.

> The man *whom* we met . . . (i.e., we met *him*.)

Whom seems to be dying out of the language, but should be kept after prepositions:

> To whom shall I send it?
> . . . for whom the bell tolls.

but not when *who* is the subject of a noun clause:

> There was some doubt about who did it.

> > **WRONG:** Thank you for inviting Joan and I to dinner.
> > **RIGHT:** Thank you for inviting Joan and *me* to dinner.

The objective case is used after all prepositions:

> **WRONG:** He gave it to John and I.
> **RIGHT:** He gave it to John and *me*.

> **WRONG:** between you and I; for you and he
> **RIGHT:** between you and *me*; for you and *him*

MIXING UP PRONOUNS
(especially *one, you, it, he,* and *they*)

➤ If you start using the word *one* you must continue with it, though it can soon result in pomposity.

> **WRONG:** One can easily spot your mistakes if you check carefully.
> **RIGHT:** One can easily spot one's mistakes if one checks carefully.

Or, better still, use *you* and *your.*

➤ Make sure, when using pronouns such as *he, she, it,* and *they,* that it is absolutely clear to whom or to what they refer.

> **WRONG:** If the baby does not like cold milk, heat it.
> **RIGHT:** Heat the milk if the baby does not like it cold.

➤ Do not confuse singular and plural.

> **WRONG:** The marigold is a fairly hardy plant; they grow in most soils.
> **RIGHT:** Marigolds are fairly hardy plants; they grow in most soils.
> **OR:** The marigold is a fairly hardy plant; it grows in most soils.

THE COMPARATIVE AND THE SUPERLATIVE

The **comparative** applies to two:

> He is the better player of the two.

The **superlative** applies to three or more:

> He is the best swimmer in the county.

> **WRONG:** John is the tallest of the two brothers.
> **RIGHT:** John is the *taller* of the two brothers.

THE PARTICIPIAL PHRASE

➤ is introduced by a verb ending in *-ing* or *-ed* and describes the noun or pronoun nearest to it, but outside the phrase itself. Such phrases are often wrongly related, or unattached.

> **WRONG:** Looking out of the window, the sun rose on our left. This means that the sun was looking out of the window.
> **RIGHT:** Looking out of the window, *we* saw the sun rise on our left.

> **WRONG:** Coming downstairs, the hall door opened. This means that the hall door was coming downstairs.
> **RIGHT:** As he was coming downstairs, the hall door opened.

> **WRONG:** A UFO was detected by searchlights flying over Disneyland.
> **RIGHT:** Flying over Disneyland, a UFO was detected by searchlights.

THE GERUND

➤ ends in *-ing* but acts as a *noun;* when qualified, it must, therefore, be preceded by an adjective (e.g., *his, her, its, my, our, your, their*):

> **WRONG:** I don't like you leaving early.
> **RIGHT:** I don't like *your* leaving early.
> (It is the *leaving* I don't like.)

> **WRONG:** I must escape without him knowing.
> **RIGHT:** I must escape without *his* knowing.

THE SUBJUNCTIVE

is rarely used now, but watch out for:

➤ Pure supposition: If I *were* king . . .

➤ After verbs of wishing: I wish she *were* here.

THE POSITION OF COMMON ADVERBS

➤ *only, just, almost, even, mainly, also*
   These should be placed immediately before the word they modify to make the meaning clear.

> She saw her uncle only when she came home on vacation. (i.e., only then did she see him)

> She saw only her uncle (and not her aunt, grandfather, etc.) when she came home on vacation.

➤ Pairings such as *both . . . and, (n) either . . . (n)or*, and *not only . . . but also* should be followed by the same part of speech or the same kind of phrase so that the construction is properly balanced.

> **WRONG:** Karen not only plays tennis but also basketball.
>
> **RIGHT:** Karen plays not only tennis but also basketball.

THE CORRECT PREPOSITION

➤ different *from* (or *to,* not *than*)

➤ to center *on, in* or *upon* (not *(a)round*)

➤ to prefer *this* to *that* (not *than*)

➤ anxious *about* (not *of*)

➤ bored *with* or *by* (not *of*)

➤ superior *to* (not *than*)

➤ cover *with* (not *by*)

MIXED CONSTRUCTIONS

➤ **Faulty comparisons**

> **WRONG:** as good if not better than . . .
>
> **RIGHT:** as good *as if* not better than . . .
>
> **OR:** at least as good as . . .

➤ **Double negatives**

> **WRONG:** I don't want nothing.
>
> **RIGHT:** I don't want *anything.*
>
> **OR:** I want nothing.

> **WRONG:** He couldn't hardly believe it.
>
> **RIGHT:** He *could* hardly believe it.

➤ **Hardly/scarcely,** when they mean *no sooner . . . than,* are followed by *when* or *before,* not *than:*

> He had *hardly/scarcely* written a page *when/before* the bell rang.

➤ **Mixed tenses**

> **WRONG:** I should be glad if you will . . .
> **RIGHT:** I should be glad if you *would* . . .
> **OR:** I *shall* be glad if you *will* . . .

> **WRONG:** I have and always will be a football fan.
> **RIGHT:** I have *been,* and always will be, a football fan.

> **WRONG:** I didn't ought to have done it.
> **RIGHT:** I *ought not to have* done it.

➤ **Order of adjectives**

> **WRONG:** the three first chapters
> (there is only one *first* chapter)
> **RIGHT:** the *first three* chapters
> (meaning chapters one, two, and three)

Chapter 3

Commonly Confused and Misused Words and Phrases

➤ **amount, number**

Use *amount* to refer to a mass or quantity: *information, rain, insecticide*. Use *number* to refer to anything that can be individually counted: *dollars, people, boxes of cereal*.

➤ **between, among**

Use *between* to refer to anything split into two or divided by two: a job divided *between* two workers. Use *among* for division by more than two: a bag of chips divided *among* a bunch of friends.

➤ **comprise**

Use *comprise* to mean *consist of, be composed of*. It does not need *of: The kit **comprised** (or was composed of) four items*.

➤ **each other, one another**

Each other refers to two people or things: In the duel they hurt *each other*. *One another* refers to more than two: The boys in the class were fighting *one another*.

➤ **different from, different than**

Men are different *from* women (not different *than*). Because the phrase *to differ than* is not English, different *than* is not standard usage.

➤ **etc.**

etc. is an abbreviation of *et cetera,* meaning "and the rest." It should not be used lazily; specify what you have in mind. Don't write *and etc., etc.,* or *e.t.c.*

➤ **imply, infer**

Use *imply* when you mean to suggest or hint, as in *His scowl **implied** disapproval.* Use *infer* to mean draw a conclusion, as in *From his scowl I **inferred** his disapproval.*

➤ **less, fewer**

Use *less* to refer to a mass or quantity: *talent, air, snow.* Use *fewer* to refer to anything that can be individually counted: *tests, airplanes, calories.*

➤ **lie, lay**

To *lie* means to put yourself in a flat position; to *lay* means to place something else (e.g., a plate) down.

To lie	*Present tenses*	I *lie* or am *lying.*
	Past tenses	I *lay* or was *lying.*
		I have *lain.*
To lay	*Present tenses*	I *lay* it or am *laying* it down.
	Past tenses	I *laid* it or was *laying* it down.
		I have *laid* it down.

➤ **like, as**

Like is a preposition or an adjective but not a conjunction. *Like* is used to introduce phrases such as *like a hero; as* is used to introduce clauses, as in *He talks as I do,* not *He talks like I do.* When you are unsure which to use, look to see whether *as* or *like* is followed by a verb. If you see one (*do* in the previous example), use *as*; otherwise use *like*, as in *He talks like me*.

➤ **literally**

Literally means exactly, to the letter, in actual fact.

> **WRONG:** He literally flew down the street.
> (He didn't sprout wings.)
> **RIGHT:** The above sentence should not be taken *literally*.

➤ **may, can**

Can means *to be able to*.
May means *have permission to*.

> I *can* swim like a fish.

> *May* I go for a swim, please?

➤ **of, off, have**

Of means belonging to or relating to. *Off* means away from or down from a place:

> He fell *off* the cliff.

> **WRONG:** I must of made a mistake.
> **RIGHT:** I must *have* made a mistake.
> *Of* is not a verb.

➤ **past, passed**

Use *passed* for the verb and its past participle; *past* for all other uses:

> He *passed* me the ball.
> He has *passed.*
> in the *past* (noun)
> he went *past* (adverb)
> in *past* ages (adjective)
> he ran *past* me (preposition)

➤ **should, would**

The main uses are the following:

– *Should*, used with all persons, also means *ought to*:

> I/you/they *should* be playing on the team.

– *Should,* also with all persons, is used for *if* clauses:

> If you *should* see him, give him my regard.

– *Would,* with all persons, expresses the idea of willingness:

> I *would* play if I could.

– *Would,* with all persons, can also mean *used to:*

> As a child he *would* play for hours.

➤ **them/those**

> **WRONG:** Give me them slippers.
> **RIGHT:** Give me *those* slippers.

➤ **try to/try and**

Normally use try *to,* except when you mean two separate actions:

> Let's *try to* make this tomorrow.
> I would like to *try and* sing it myself this time.

➤ **unique**
Unique means the only one of its kind—e.g., the phoenix. Strictly, things can't be *quite unique* or *very unique.* Likewise with *invaluable,* which means priceless.

➤ **who, which, that**
These three words are relative pronouns used to introduce subordinate clauses, as in *Nan is the engineer **who** designed the bridge.* People should be introduced with *who. That* and *which* are reserved for things, as in *This is the bridge **that** Nan designed.* Therefore, avoid usages as *The person **which** designed the bridge is an engineer.*

WORDS OFTEN CONFUSED

Additional words sometimes cause confusion because they look or sound very much like other words:

accept	to receive
except	to omit, exclude; not including
adapt	to adjust
adopt	to accept and approve, take as one's own
affect (verb)	to influence or produce an effect on
effect (noun or verb)	a result; to bring about or accomplish
aggravate	to make worse
irritate	to annoy, exasperate
air	the mixture of gases that surrounds the earth
heir	one who inherits, a beneficiary

alibi	a fact or claim that one was elsewhere
excuse	an apology offered

allowed	permitted
aloud	audibly, loudly

allusion (to)	a casual or indirect reference
illusion	a false impression or image; a magician's trick
delusion	a deception, mistaken belief

already	by this time
all ready	all persons (things) are ready

altogether	completely
all together	all in one place

altar	a place for worship
alter	to change

always	ever, constantly
all ways	all directions or methods

amount	How much? (weight or money)
number	How many? (individual items)

ascent	an upward climb
assent	to agree, agreement

astrology	foretelling the future by the stars
astronomy	science of the planets and stars

bail	security for a court appearance
bale	a bundle

bare	naked; to uncover
bear	to carry; an animal

base	a basis, support
bass	a low deep tone; a fish

beach	a shore
beech	a tree
berth	a sleeping place, a bunk
birth	the act of being born
beside	at the side of
besides	in addition to
bloc	a group of nations acting as a unit
block	a piece of material; an obstacle
board	a plank, table; to receive meals; to go on board
bored	weary with tediousness; made a hole
born	to come into the world by birth
borne	carried, endured
borough	an incorporated town
burro	a donkey
burrow	a hole in which an animal lives; (to) excavate
brake	to put the brakes on (e.g., a car)
break	to shatter; an interval
breath	air drawn into lungs
breathe	to draw air into lungs
bridal	pertaining to a wedding or the bride
bridle	a device to control a horse; to curb, restrain
Britain	the country
Briton	the inhabitant
broach	to open (e.g., a subject for discussion)
brooch	an ornament

cannon	a gun
canon	a churchman; church law
canvas	coarse cloth for tent
canvass	to solicit votes, orders
capital	chief; punishable by death; the chief city of a state or country; a sum of money
capitol	the building in which the legislature meets
carat	a measure of the weight of a precious stone
caret	a proofreader's mark to indicate an insertion
carrot	a vegetable
karat	a measure of the purity of gold
cede	to yield, surrender
seed	a spore, egg, sperm
cereal	a breakfast food
serial	in a sequence; a story told in parts
ceremonial	of a ritual or ceremony; formal
ceremonious	too much concerned with formalities, showy
choose	present tense of *to choose*
chose	past tense of *to choose*
cite	mention, refer to
sight	vision; something that is seen
site	position, location
civic	of a city
civil	polite; not military (e.g., civil service)

climactic	of a climax
climatic	of climate
clothes	garments
cloths	pieces of cloth
coarse	rough, harsh, crude
course	path, route (e.g., for racing, golf); the division of a meal; a series; "of course"
compare	to point out similarities
contrast	to point out differences
complement	that which makes up or completes
compliment	praise
contemporary	existing at the same time as
modern	up-to-date
contemptible	vile, mean
contemptuous	showing or feeling scorn
continual	frequent, repeated (e.g., dripping tap)
continuous	connected, unbroken (e.g., stream of water)
core	the hard center of fruit
corps	a unit of soldiers or other persons
council	an assembly
counsel	advice; legal adviser; to advise
credible	believable
creditable	deserving praise
credulous	inclined to believe; gullible
currant	small berry
current	now running, in general use; flow of water, electricity, air

decease	death
disease	illness
defective	faulty
deficient	lacking
defer	postpone
differ	be unlike
definite	fixed, certain, clear
definitive	final, complete, thorough
deprecate	to express disapproval of
depreciate	to go down in value, rate less highly
desert	barren place; that which is deserved; to abandon
dessert	sweet course in a meal
detract (from)	to lessen, take away from
distract	to divert (attention)
diner	one who eats; a restaurant
dinner	a meal
disburse	to pay out money
disperse	to scatter, spread (or vanish)
discover	to find something that was always there
invent	to create or devise something new
discreet	prudent, wary
discrete	separate, unconnected
disinterested	neutral, unbiased
uninterested	lacking interest, not interested
dose	quantity of medicine to be taken at one time
doze	to sleep

dual	double, composed of two
duel	a fight between two people
dyeing	coloring
dying	almost dead
economic	of finances
economical	careful, thrifty
effective	having an effect; coming into operation
effectual	answering its purpose
efficacious	sure to produce the desired effect
efficient	competent; working productively
elicit	to draw out
illicit	not legal
eligible	fit to be chosen
illegible	indecipherable
emigrant	one who leaves the country
immigrant	one who enters the country
eminent	prominent, distinguished
imminent	threatening; near at hand
envelop	to surround or cover
envelope	a flat wrapper for a letter or a thin package
especially	notably, particularly
specially	for a special occasion or purpose
exceptionable	objectionable
exceptional	unusual
fact	a truth, actual happening
factor	a contributory element, cause

faint	to swoon; dim, indistinct, weak
feint	sham attack or blow; to pretend to do something

fatal	resulting in death
fateful	deciding one's fate

flaunt	to show off
flout	to treat with scorn

flea	an insect
flee	to run away

flew	past tense of *to fly*; to soar
flu	influenza
flue	chimney, smokestack

flowed	past participle of *to flow* (water)
flown	past participle of *to fly* (birds)

foregoing	preceding, gone before
forgoing	giving up, abstaining from

formally	in a formal manner
formerly	previously

fortuitous	happening by chance
fortunate	having or bringing good luck

foul	dirty, bad-smelling
fowl	a bird

gait	a manner of walking, e.g., sauntering
gate	a means of entering or leaving

genteel	affectedly elegant
gentle	not rough

guerilla	raiding soldier
gorilla	ape

hanged	executed ("hanged by the neck")
hung	other uses of the verb *to hang*
heal	to mend
heel	part of the foot
hear	to perceive sound, listen to
here	at this place
hoard	a hidden stockpile
horde	a crowd, multitude
human	of man as opposed to animal or god
humane	compassionate, kind
idle	unoccupied, unemployed
idol	an object of worship; a dearly beloved or admired person
idyll (idyl)	a pastoral or romantic work
illegible	indecipherable
ineligible	not fit to be chosen
imaginary	of a thing that exists only in the imagination
imaginative	having a high degree of imagination
imperial	of an empire or emperor
imperious	proud, domineering
imply	to hint (speaker implies)
infer	to draw a conclusion (hearer infers)
impracticable	that cannot be put into effect
impractical	not having practical skill; not suited to actual conditions
industrial	of industry
industrious	hardworking

ingenious	skillful in inventing
ingenuous	artless, innocent
intellectual	of the mind, having superior powers of reasoning; a person who is concerned with things of the mind (as opposed to feelings)
intelligent	clever
intelligible	clear, understandable
into	entering, inside (e.g., He went into the house.)
in to	separate senses (e.g., She came in to tell us the news.)
it's	it is (or it has)
its	belonging to it
judicial	connected with a judge or law court
judicious	having sound judgment
larva	immature form (e.g., caterpillar)
lava	from a volcano
lead	metal; present tense of *to lead*
led	past tense of *to lead*
less	smaller in amount
fewer	smaller in number
lightening	making less heavy or less dark
lightning	a flash of
liqueur	strong, sweet alcoholic drink
liquor	any alcoholic drink
loath/loth	reluctant, unwilling
loathe	to dislike greatly

| loose | to unfasten; not tight |
| lose | to fail to win; fail to keep |

| luxuriant | growing profusely |
| luxurious | very comfortable; self-indulgent |

| marshal | officer; to arrange in due order |
| martial | of war or the army (court-martial) |

| masterful | imperious, domineering |
| masterly | expert, skillful |

| maybe | perhaps |
| may be | e.g., it may be . . . |

| momentary | short-lived |
| momentous | important |

| moral | right, virtuous; a lesson from a story |
| morale | mental state of confidence |

| negligent | careless |
| negligible | small or unimportant |

| new | opposite of old |
| knew | past tense of *to know* |

| notable | worth noting |
| noticeable | easy to see, prominent |

| observance | obeying, paying heed to (a rule or custom) |
| observation | noting, looking at |

| official | connected with an office; authorized |
| officious | meddlesome |

oral	spoken (of the mouth)
aural	pertaining to the ear
verbal	in words (spoken or written)

palate	the roof of the mouth
palette	an artist's board for mixing colors
pallet	a cot, bunk, berth
partake of	to take or share (food or rest)
participate in	to take part in
passed	past tense of *to pass;* went by
past	a former time; beyond
peace	opposite of war; quiet
piece	a portion or part
pedal	a foot lever
peddle	to sell
persecute	to oppress, harass
prosecute	to take legal proceedings against
personal	individual, private
personnel	employees or staff
plain	flat country; clear; undecorated; unattractive
plane	level surface; to shave level; tool; tree; airplane
pray	to worship, beg
prey	hunted animal; plunder
precede	to go before in arrangement or rank
proceed	to go along, continue
precedence	the act or fact of preceding; priority
precedents	examples, models, standards
precipitate	hasty, rash
precipitous	steep

prescribe	to order, lay down as a rule
proscribe	to condemn, prohibit
principal	chief, most important
principle	truth, law, idea; code of conduct
profit	financial gain
prophet	religious forecaster
quiet	silent
quite	fairly, very, completely
rain	water from the clouds; to fall as water
reign	to rule
rein	to check, restrain
raise(d)	to lift, make grow, increase
raze	to demolish, level to the ground
rise (rose)	to get up or go up
recourse	"to have recourse to" (to resort to)
resource	source of supply; device; ingenuity
re-cover	to cover again
recover	to regain health, regain possession of
reek	to smell strongly, to give an impression
wreak	to inflict damage
re-form	to form again
reform	to correct, improve
re-sign	to sign again
resign	to give up (e.g., a job or office)
respectable	worthy of respect
respectful	showing respect
respective	relating to each in order
review	survey, inspection
revue	a stage production

right	opposite of left or wrong; just claim or due
rite	ceremony (religious)
wright	a workman (e.g., playwright)
write	to put words on paper

rogue	a villain
rouge	a cosmetic for coloring the cheeks red

rout	a defeat
route	a course, way, or road for passage or travel; to direct

scarce	of ordinary things temporarily not plentiful
rare	of things infrequent at all times

seasonable	suitable to the occasion or season
seasonal	occurring at a particular season

sensible	showing good sense
sensitive	capable of feeling deeply; responsive to slight changes

sensual	indulging the senses
sensuous	relating to the senses

sew	i.e., with a needle
sow	i.e., with seeds

shear	to shave, cut
sheer	steep; absolute; transparent; to swerve

sight	thing seen; faculty of vision
site	location, position, plot

soar	to fly high
sore	painful

sociable	enjoying company
social	pertaining to society
solidarity	show of support for, holding the same interest as
solidity	state of being firm, stable, or solid
staid	sedate, sober
stayed	past tense of *to stay*; remained
stalactite	comes down from "ceiling" of a cave
stalagmite	grows up from the ground
stationary	not moving
stationery	writing materials
stimulant	alcohol, drug
stimulus	incentive
straight	not bent, direct
strait(s)	narrow places, difficulties
suit	fit; set of clothes or cards
suite	a number of things forming a series or set (e.g., rooms, furniture)
superficial	on the surface, shallow
superfluous	too many, more than is needed
taught	past tense of *to teach*
taut	tight, tense
temporal	earthly (as opposed to spiritual or eternal)
temporary	not permanent
their	belonging to them
there	in that place; "there is"
they're	they are

threw	past tense of *to throw*
through	from one end or side to the other; by means of
thorough	complete, in detail; very careful
to	always used except for:
too	also or in an excessive degree ("too hot")
two	number
translucent	allowing light through but not transparent
transparent	that can be seen through
urban	of a town
urbane	well-bred, suave, civilized
vain	conceited
vane	a wind indicator, weathercock
vein	a blood vessel
vial	a small bottle
vile	disgusting, morally repulsive
vice	evil, wickedness
vise	a tool for holding
vicious	cruel
viscous	thick and gluey
waist	a part of the body
waste	rubbish, barren land
waive	to set aside, forgo (a claim, right, rule)
wave	shake or move to and fro; curve(s) of water, hair, sound, heat, etc.
weather	sunshine, wind, rain, etc.
whether	if

were	past tense of *to be*
we're	we are
where	in what place?

| who's | who is (or has) |
| whose | belonging to whom |

| yoke | a bar or frame to join two work animals |
| yolk | the yellow part of an egg |

| your | belonging to you |
| you're | you are |

Chapter 4

Spelling and Punctuation

Some people are natural spellers. They see a word once or twice, and it sticks in their memory. Others master spelling by studying and practice. Still others may memorize words on a list, but when they write the words, the spelling comes out wrong. Brain researchers still don't know why this happens. They believe that spelling talent has little to do with intelligence, however. Many brilliant people are hopeless spellers.

Wide, attentive reading will help. Careful pronunciation and grouping of words in families may also be beneficial, as will dividing words into syllables, thereby spelling words part by part. Another method that helps is studying word parts, namely *prefixes, suffixes*, *roots,* and *stems*.

Prefixes

A prefix is the name of a group of letters at the beginning of some words that help convey the meaning of the word. You can't speak English without using words that contain prefixes, such as

re meaning *again*, as in *re*peat, *re*read, and *re*visit
co meaning *together*, as in *co*operate and
co-captain
mis meaning *bad* or *improper*, as in *mis*take and
*mis*demeanor

Suffixes

Suffixes, like prefixes, also convey meaning, but suffixes are found at the ends of words such as

> -*ism* meaning *belief*, as in extrem*ism*, liberal*ism*, and monothe*ism*
>
> -*er* or -*eer* or *or*, meaning *a person who*, as in mountain*eer* (a person who climbs mountains) and sail*or* (a person who sails)

Roots and Stems

A great many words also contain roots or stems. Roots are word parts that originated in other languages, mostly Latin and Greek, that have been absorbed by English. Stems are a variety of roots that have evolved into new forms. Both stems and roots convey meaning—just as though they were prefixes or suffixes. For example:

> *tempor*, meaning *time*, as in temporary (for a short time) and contemporary (at the same time)
>
> *terr*, meaning *land*, as in terrestrial (of the earth) and subterranean (underground)

There are literally hundreds of prefixes, suffixes, roots, and stems. Knowing many of them can help you figure out how to spell unfamiliar words.

SPELLING RULES

But you will gain the most by becoming acquainted with the basic spelling rules—which happen not to be "rules" in the strict sense of the word. Because English spelling grew haphazardly, the rules are merely observations of patterns that developed over time.

To improve your spelling, study and use the following guidelines:

1. Use *i* before *e* except after *c*, if the sound is *ee*.

➤ If the sound is *ee*, use *i-e*, as in:

> ach*ie*ve, bel*ie*ve, s*ie*ge, f*ie*ld, rel*ie*f, and n*ie*ce,

except after *c*, as in

> c*ei*ling, rec*ei*ve, dec*ei*t, perc*ei*ve, and conc*ei*t

Exceptions:

> *either, leisure, caffeine, protein, seize, weird, counterfeit, plebeian, species,* and *financier*

➤ If the sound in NOT *ee*, use *e-i*, as in:

> n*ei*ghbor, h*ei*ght, w*ei*gh, w*ei*ght, for*ei*gn, and h*ei*r

Exceptions:

> *friend, sieve, mischief,* and *handkerchief*

2. When adding a prefix to a word, the spelling of the base word remains unchanged. For example:

dis	+	appear	=	disappear
mis	+	spell	=	misspell
un	+	natural	=	unnatural
inter	+	relate	=	interrelate
over	+	rule	=	overrule
with	+	hold	=	withhold

➤ When a prefix adapts to the first letter of the base word or root, use a double letter, as in ad + tract (draw) = *attract*; ir + regular = *irregular*, and in such words as *appoint, announce, correspond, collect, illegal, immortal, occur, oppose, suffer,* and *suppose.*

3. When adding a suffix that begins with a consonant, the spelling of the base word remains the same. For example:

sad	+ ness	=	sadness
hope	+ less	=	hopeless
care	+ ful	=	careful

Also:

excitement, meanness, drunkenness, government

➤ With base words ending in *y*, the *y* is usually changed to *i* before the suffix is added:

happiness, loneliness, beautifully, and *happily*

Exception: one-syllable words ending in *y*, such as

dryness and *shyly*

➤ When adding an *ly* ending to turn an adjective into an adverb, normally just add *ly,* as in *extreme + ly = extremely*, *definite + ly = definitely*, *careful + ly = carefully*, *beautiful + ly = beautifully*, and *accidental + ly = accidentally*.

➤ Words ending in *-ic* form adverbs by adding *-ally*, as in *basically*, *terrifically*, and *fantastically*.

Exception:

publicly.

➤ Words ending in *y* preceded by a consonant change the *y* to *i*, as in *happy—happily* and *necessary—necessarily*.

➤ Words ending in *-ble* and *-ple* drop the *e*, as in *probable—probably* and *simple—simply*.

➤ Words ending in *-ue* drop the *e* and add *ly*, as in *true—truly* and *due—duly*.

4. In words of one syllable ending in a single vowel followed by a single consonant, double the final letter of the base word. For example:

> *tap—tapping, hop—hopping, scar—scarred, spar—sparring*

➤ Words ending in a silent *e* drop the *e*, as in *stare— staring, spare—spared, come—coming, excite— exciting, argue—arguing.*

Exceptions:

– Words ending in *-oe:*

> *canoeing, hoeing*

– Words ending in *-ce* and *-ge*:

> *notice—noticeable, manage—manageable, courage—courageous*
> (The *e* keeps the sound "soft" like *j* and *s.*)

– Words ending in *-ic* or *-ac* insert a *k* before the *-ing:*

> *picnic—picnicking, panic—panicked, traffic—trafficker*

5. In words of more than one syllable that end in one vowel and one consonant (such as *happen, occur, prefer, commit*) double the consonant before adding *-ing, -ed, -able, -er* **only** when the emphasis falls on the last vowel. For example:

> *begin—beginning, refer—referring, occur— occurring, regret—regrettable, forget—forgettable*

➤ Do not double the consonant if the emphasis shifts, as in *prefer—preference*, and not before the suffixes *-ity* and *-ize*, as in *equality—equalize.*

➤ Do not double the consonant if the emphasis is any-
where but on the last syllable before the suffix, as in
happen—happening, offer—offered, travel—traveler.

Exceptions:

> *handicapped, kidnapped*

6. To turn singular nouns into plurals, add *s*, as in
dog—dogs and *picture—pictures*. After *s, x, ch, sh,*
and *z*, add *-es*, as in *dress—dresses* and *sex—sexes*.

➤ If the noun ends in a consonant followed by *y*, drop the
y and add *ies*, as in *liberty—liberties, monastery—
monasteries, lady—ladies, story—stories, ally—allies*.

➤ If the noun ends in a vowel followed by *y*, simply add
s, as in *donkey—donkeys, valley—valleys, chimney—
chimneys, boy—boys, tray—trays*.

➤ For nouns ending in *i*, add *s*, as in *alibis* and *rabbis*.

➤ For nouns ending in *o*, add *s*, as in *pianos, dynamos,
photos*.

Exceptions:

> *tomatoes, potatoes, heroes, mosquitoes, echoes,
> mottoes, torpedoes, cargoes, volcanoes, vetoes,
> embargoes, tornadoes, dominoes, buffaloes,
> desperadoes, haloes, noes.*

➤ Some nouns ending in *f* and *fe* are made plural by turn-
ing the *f* to *v* before adding *s*, as in *calf—calves, wife—
wives, knife—knives, half—halves, shelf—shelves,
thief—thieves, loaf—loaves*. Some such words may be
spelled either way: *hoofs—hooves, wharfs—wharves*.

➤ Some English nouns of foreign origin have slight spelling changes, as in *crisis—crises, oasis—oases, criterion—criteria, phenomenon—phenomena, alumnus—alumni, larva—larvae, medium—media, ox—oxen.*

➤ Plurals of hyphenated compound nouns usually add the *s* to the main noun part, as in *passers-by* and *mothers-in-law.*

➤ Some nouns have the same form in both singular and plural, as in *sheep, aircraft, moose, deer, fish,* and *swine.*

➤ For some nouns, the difference between the singular and plural form lies in their vowels, as in *foot—feet, goose—geese, man—men, tooth—teeth,* and *woman—women.*

THE MOST COMMONLY MISSPELLED WORDS

The list that follows, consisting of what are sometimes called "spelling demons," are the most popular words to misspell. As you will see, many of them violate basic spelling guidelines.

➤ **a lot**
A lot is two words, not one. *A lot* of people make this mistake. *A lot* of writers frown on using *a lot* in formal prose.

➤ **acquaintance**
The *ance* ending gives some people trouble, but more people stumble over the *c* after the initial *a*. The rule is that only words referring to water, as in *aqueduct* and *aquatic* begin with *a-q*. All others include *c* between the *a* and the *q*, as in *acquaint* and *acquiesce.*

➤ **affect-effect**

Affect is a verb, *effect* is a noun (with one exception). Spelling *affect* (verb) when you mean *effect* (noun) will *affect* your reputation as a proficient speller. The exception: when *effect* means to bring to pass or to accomplish, as in:

> Study hard to *effect* a change in your spelling performance.

➤ **all right, already, altogether**

All right is two words; it's never one. It's different from *already* and *altogether*, which may be either one word or two, depending on their meaning. Remember that, and you'll be *all right*.

Already is one word unless used in the sense of:

> We are *all ready* to take the spelling quiz.

Altogether is also one word except when referring to a group as in:

> The team met *all together* before the game.

Otherwise, *altogether* means thoroughly or completely, as in:

> Spelling is altogether too complicated.

➤ **athlete**

Because *athlete* is often pronounced *ath-a-lete*, as though the word contains three syllables, some people spell it "athelete."

➤ **cloths, clothes**

No one would mistakenly put on cloths instead of clothes in the morning, so why is *cloths* mistakenly spelled *clothes*, and vice versa?

➤ **conscience, conscious, conscientious**

Conscience, made up of *con* and *science*, means a sense of moral righteousness.

Conscious, the opposite of *unconscious*, means being mentally awake.

Conscientious looks like a blend of *conscience* and *conscious*. It means hard-working, an attribute of a *conscientious* speller.

➤ **coarse, course**

Coarse, an adjective, describes something rough, harsh, or crude. *Course*, a noun, names a path, a route, the division of a meal, and, of course, something you take in school.

➤ **could've (could of), could have**

Could've is a marriage of two verbs, *could* and *have*. The phrase *could of* is sometimes mistaken for *could have*. But *could of* is not standard English. Don't use it or its cousins: *should of, might of, would of*. Instead, write *should have, might have*, and *would have*.

➤ **desert, dessert**

This spelling demon may remind you of your third-grade teacher, who may have told you that, because kids like two helpings of *dessert*, spell the word with two *s*'s.

➤ **doesn't**

Doesn't combines *does* and *not*. The apostrophe takes the place of the *o* in not. Because that's the only difference between spelling *does not* and *doesn't*, it makes little sense to write *dosen't* or *doesnt*.

➤ **etc.**

Etc. is the abbreviation for *et cetera*, used when subsequent items on a list are too obvious to spell out, as in

1, 2, 3, 4, *etc.* Because *etc.* is an abbreviation, it is always followed by a period, even in mid-sentence. Why so many people write *ect.* is a puzzle.

➤ **its, it's**

It's combines *it* and *is*. That's the only way *it's* correct. *Its* (without the apostrophe) indicates possession. One would never write *his's* or *her's*, so don't write *it's* unless it means *it is*.

➤ **jewelry**

Mispronunciation lies at the core of why *jewelry* is often misspelled *jewlery* or *jewelery*.

➤ **judgment, judgement**

This word is a gift from the spelling god. Both versions are perfectly acceptable.

➤ **loneliness**

Anyone who writes *lonliness* has forgotten to keep the final *-e* before a suffix beginning with a consonant. Writing *ninty* instead of *ninety* breaks the same rule.

➤ **lose, loose**

One *o* makes a difference. Don't confuse *lose*, which you can do when you make a bet, with *loose*, which rhymes with *goose*. Be careful with *loose* change in your pocket, or you might *lose* it.

➤ **lead, led**

Because the metal known as lead is pronounced "led," the past tense of the verb *to lead*, *led* is sometimes mistakenly spelled *lead*.

➤ **lovable**

Lovable exemplifies the rule that says drop the final *-e* before a suffix beginning with a vowel. Therefore, write *lovable* instead of *loveable* and *arguing* instead of *argueing.* There are exceptions, however, such as *mileage, noticeable,* and *knowledgeable.*

➤ **misspell**
Misspell has two *-s*'s because the prefix *mis-* is added to the verb *spell.* Remember that prefixes are kept intact even when their final letter is the same as the first letter of the base word, as in *unnecessary, cooperate, sub-basement,* and so on.

➤ **nuclear**
Because so many prominent people, including presidents, say *nuc-u-lar,* when they mean *nuc-le-ar,* the word has become troublesome.

➤ **occasion, occasionally**
Both *occasion* and *occasionally* have two *c*'s and only one *s.* Don't sneak in a double *s.* One is enough.

➤ **perform**
Because *pre-* is a common prefix, it precedes many words, as *predict, prevent, prejudice. Pre* means before, as in *prewar* (before the war). *Perform* is unrelated. Why the word is often spelled *preform* remains a mystery worth pondering.

➤ **precede**
Exceed, succeed, and *proceed* all end with the letters *-eed. Precede* is not one of them. Therefore, don't write *preceed.*

➤ **prejudice, prejudiced**
Prejudice is a noun. Its derivative *prejudiced* is an adjective. The two words are not interchangeable. A *prejudiced* person suffers from *prejudice.*

➤ **principal, principle**
In grade school you may have been told that the *principal* is your pal. That's why you spell the word

principal. One might hope that principals have noble *principles*, but that is not always the case. As an adjective, *principal* means most important or highest.

➤ **professor, profession**
Professors are sometimes called "Prof," a title with one *f*, the grade one deserves for spelling *professor* and *profession* with two.

➤ **psychology**
The *p* in *psychology* throws some people. Also, because of the *h* some people confuse the word with *physiology*, which relates to the body, not the mind.

➤ **quite, quiet**
Each word contains the same letters, but *quite*, meaning rather or very, means something quite different from *quiet*, or silent.

➤ **rhythm**
Rhythm is difficult to spell because the *h* after *r* is silent. Just remember that the *h* appears twice.

➤ **schedule**
Schedule is a two-syllable word sometimes given a third by those who pronounce it *sched-u-al* and spell it as they hear it—*schedual.* If pronounced *sched-yule*, it will probably be spelled as it should.

➤ **separate**
Look for *a rat* in *separate*, and you'll never go wrong.

➤ **similar**
Because *similar* resembles familiar, people often write *similiar*. Don't let the similarity between the two words confuse you.

➤ **supposed to, used to**

Supposed is the past tense of the verb *suppose*. Because the past tense of many verbs end with the letter *d*, don't write *suppose to* or *use to*.

➤ **than, then**

When making a comparison (Phil eats faster *than* Fido), use *than* instead of *then*. *Then* is a time word, like *when*. Both contain the letter *e*.

➤ **there, their, they're**

Don't confuse these three words. Each has its own separate use and meaning.

There is the opposite of *here*. Both are places. *There* are many places to use this word. *Their* indicates possession: *Their* spelling is getting better all the time. *They're* combines *they* and *are*. *They're* words that can easily be combined.

➤ **through**

This word is a demon because it resembles *though* and *thorough*. Above all, avoid *thru*, as in *thru-way*, a sample of commercial jargon like *lite* for *light* and *e-z* for *easy*.

➤ **tragedy**

Isn't it sad that writers sometimes add an extra *d* to tragedy? If you write *tradgedy*, it's no *tragedy*, but it is dead wrong.

➤ **villain**

Villain is a treacherous word to spell because people mistakenly use the *i-a* combination found in such words as *brilliant* and *Machiavellian* instead of the *a-i* found in *pain* and *gain*.

➤ **weather, whether**

Whether it rains or shines, neither *weather* nor *whether* is ever spelled *wheather*.

➤ **Wednesday**

The first *d* in *Wednesday* causes problems because it is silent. Most people have no trouble abbreviating the third day of the week, *Wed.*, but when it comes to spelling the whole word, the third letter, *d*, falls into fourth place or is left out altogether.

➤ **who's, whose**

Like every contraction, *who's* combines two words, *who* and *is*, as in Who's not going to misspell *who's* anymore? *Whose*, on the other hand, is a pronoun indicating possession, as in You're the person *whose* spelling is bound to improve.

➤ **woman, women**

It's odd that few people err when it comes to spelling *man* and *men*, but when the gender changes, they make a mess of spelling *woman* and *women*.

PUNCTUATION— THE PERIOD

➤ Periods are used to mark the end of statements. The statement may consist of only one word as in greetings like "Hello," commands like "Stop," and replies like "No."

➤ Periods also follow abbreviations, as in *Ms., Nov., Ave., Inc., etc., i.e.,* and *a.m.*

CAPITAL LETTERS ARE USED

➤ at the beginning of every sentence.

➤ at the beginning of a passage of direct quotation (see page 63).

➤ for proper nouns (i.e., names of *particular* persons, places, things), and for months of the year and days of the week:

> Darnell, Everest, Oklahoma, July, Monday

➤ for adjectives derived from proper nouns, especially places and people:

> English, French, Jeffersonian, Elizabethan

➤ for the first and all main words in *any kind of title:* plays, poems, books, TV programs, films

> *Far from the Madding Crowd*
> *The Way We Were*

newspapers and magazines

> *Time*

names of ships, houses, inns, a person's title

> Governor of New York

the titles of institutions and businesses

> Women's Institute

➤ at the beginning of each line of verse (except in some modern poetry).

➤ for the pronoun *I*.

➤ when a noun is personified or considered as a grand abstract idea:

> "The Child is Father of the Man."

➤ for *He* and *His* when referring to God.

THE QUESTION MARK

Is used for all direct questions:

> What are you doing?
> You will come, won't you?

but *not* for reported questions:

> I wonder what he is doing.
> Ask him who did it.

Don't forget the question mark at the end of a long question.

THE EXCLAMATION MARK

➤ expresses some kind of astonishment or a sharp outburst or comment:

> Fire! Fire!

It can also add a tone of humor or sarcasm:

> And he was supposed to be an expert!

Don't overuse it and don't use more than one at a time.

COMMAS

The following rules cover the main uses. You will find
that there are many other optional uses that lend
emphasis or give a finer point of meaning.

Commas are used

➤ to separate words, phrases, or clauses in a list:

– a series of nouns:
His room was littered with books, pens, papers,
and maps.

– a series of adjectives:

He was a quiet, gentle, unassuming man.

When one adjective describes the other or when the
last adjective is closely linked with its noun, there
should be no comma:

the deep blue sky; a new state college
(Contrast: a thin, white hand)

– a series of adverbs:

Try to work quickly, confidently, and efficiently.

– a series of phrases:

We spent an enjoyable day visiting the zoo, rowing
on the lake, and picnicking in the park.

– a series of verbs or clauses:

He started running, slipped on the wet grass, and
landed short of the sandpit.

It is better with larger groupings to put a comma before
the *and*.

The comma is also used between two long main clauses joined by *and* or *but,* especially when the subjects of the clauses are different.

➤ before and after a phrase or clause in apposition (i.e., when placing a group of words after a noun to give a fuller explanation or description of it):

> Ashley, *Bill's older sister,* brought home a new hat, *a pink one with feathers.*

➤ to separate transitional words and phrases that show the link between the whole sentence and the preceding one(s):

> however, on the other hand, moreover

> They tried hard. The conditions, *however,* were against them.

➤ to set off the person(s) addressed or called to whether by name or other description:

> Look out, *Fred!* Now, *you fool,* you've missed it!

➤ to set off insertions or afterthoughts. Dashes or parentheses may also be used for this.

Use commas on either side of the parenthetical expression:

> Sunday, *as everyone knows,* is a day of rest.

➤ to mark off interjections—words like *yes, no, please:*

> *Well, er, no,* I don't think I will, *thank you.*

➤ before adding clauses like *don't you?* or *isn't it?*:

> They played well, *didn't they?*

➤ to mark off a participial phrase:

> *Sensing danger,* she reversed the car.

➤ to mark off adverbial clauses, especially when they start the sentence, except when they are very short. Adverbial clauses are introduced by words like *although, if, because:*

> *Although you may not realize it,* you have been moody lately.

➤ to mark off an adjective clause that merely comments but does not limit or define:

> The boys, *who were talking loudly,* were punished.

Without commas this would mean that *only* the boys who were talking loudly were punished; *with* commas it means that *all* the boys were talking loudly, and were punished. The commas act like brackets.

NOTE: Don't put a comma between the subject and its verb:

> **WRONG:**   What he wrote, was illegible.
> **RIGHT:**   What he wrote was illegible.

PUNCTUATING CONVERSATION/DIRECT QUOTATIONS

➤ Start a new paragraph *every* time the speaker changes.

➤ The words spoken and the accompanying punctuation are enclosed in quotation marks.

...ay also be used

...aking off a sentence for an abrupt change of
...r when adding another construction:

...following day we had better luck—but that is
...ther story.

...nasize a repeated word:

...e new regime imposed rigid laws—laws that the
...plice found difficult to enforce.

...bringing together a number of items:

...Toothbrush, can opener, matches, soap pads—
...these are often forgotten by inexperienced
...campers.

...ignify missing letters:

D--- it!

...rentheses (always two) are, like dashes, used for
...ides and for enclosing additional information:

Citrus fruits (oranges, lemons, limes) are rich in
vitamin C.

Parentheses, like dashes, often carry the meaning of
that is [i.e.] or *namely*.

If there is a parenthetical *phrase* at the end of a
sentence, the period follows the parenthesis; if the
parentheses enclose a *sentence*, the period comes
inside.

NOTE: The punctuation comes *inside* the quotation
marks.

➤ Even though the words spoken would form a sentence
on their own, they are followed by a comma (not a
period) when the verb and its subject come *afterwards*:

"We are going away," they said.

but "Where are you going?" he asked.

➤ When the subject and verb start the sentence, they are
followed by a comma, and the first word spoken has a
capital letter:

They said, "We are going away."

➤ When the quotation is interrupted to insert the verb and
its subject, one comma is needed when breaking off the
speech and another immediately before continuing it.
The next word within the quotation marks has a small
letter, because it is continuing the quoted sentence:

"I am not," he stressed, "particularly happy about
this."

Consider the following two sentences:

"I am going," he said. "Do not try to stop me."

QUOTATION MARKS ARE ALSO USED

➤ when quoting someone's words or from a book:

"To be, or not to be" begins a famous speech from
Hamlet.

Take care, when quoting from a book/play/poem, that
your own sentence leads naturally into the quotation.

➤ when using foreign words, jargon, specialist words or slang; or to show that a word is used sarcastically. In print these might be italicized.

THE APOSTROPHE IS USED

➤ to denote *possession* with nouns. The singular noun takes an apostrophe followed by an *s.* Plurals ending in s add an apostrophe after the final *s:*

> a lady's hat, the ladies' hats (the hats of the ladies)
>
> a week's vacation, six weeks' vacation
>
> the glass's rim, Dickens's novels, Charles's sister
>
> Jones's cap, the Joneses' house (i.e., the house of the Joneses)

Be careful with unusual plurals like men, children, mice which are treated as if they were singular:

> men's coats, women's rights, children's toys (*never* write mens' or childrens')

For proper nouns ending in a sounded *e* and an *s* or in *s* vowel *s* (e.g., Euripides, Moses) add the apostrophe after the *s:*

> Ulysses' adventures, Archimedes' principle, Jesus' mother
>
> Note also—for goodness' sake.

In units involving two or more nouns or in a compound noun or phrase, put the apostrophe on the last word only:

> William and Mary's reign, my father-in-law's house

This does not apply

> my brother's and

NOTE: The apostroph
yours, hers, our
belonging to it).
(belonging to one

➤ to indicate a *contraction.* T
where the letter(s) has(have

> didn't, can't, they're (the
> I'll, it's (meaning it is or it

But note: shan't, won't.

➤ for the plural form of certain *let*
although this apostrophe is now

> the three R's, P's and Q's, if's

➤ Don't use the apostrophe in ordinar
where there is no idea of ownership.

> The store sells potatoes, beans,

DASHES AND PARENT

Dashes are used when breaking off a sent
an afterthought or an explanatory commer
list:

> In August last year—I was with my famil
> time—I had a serious accident.
>
> Nothing—food, plates, cutlery, pans—coul
> unattended.

Dashes m

➤ when bre
thought

> The
> and

➤ to emp

> Th
> p

➤ when

➤ to s

> Pa
> as

HYPHENS AND UNHYPHENATED WORDS

The tendency is for commonly used compounds, especially those formed with a prefix, to be single, unhyphenated words, e.g., antiwar, midterm, multistory, prerecorded, reexamined. The hyphen is, however, used in the following cases:

➤ when the prefix is followed by a proper name:

mid-Atlantic, pre-Raphaelite, un-American

➤ when the prefix is stressed and might be confused with a twin compound:

re-sign, re-cover, re-form, un-ionized (contrast resign, recover, reform, unionized)

➤ when the compound forms an adjective *followed by* a noun, especially when confusion would result:

fifty-odd people (contrast fifty odd people), an ill-educated man, a fast-moving car, an out-of-work mechanic, a poverty-stricken family

➤ when the compound is formed from a phrase, especially one containing a preposition:

mother-in-law, bumper-to-bumper, devil-may-care attitude

➤ for compound numbers between 21 and 99 (e.g., sixty-four) to denote "up to and including" in numbers and dates (e.g., 1980-1990), and for fractions used as adjectives (e.g., a two-thirds majority).

The hyphen also occurs in some compounds when the end of the first part of the compound has the same letter as the beginning of the next part, e.g., co-op, short-term.

THE SEMICOLON IS, OR MAY BE, USED

➤ to separate clauses that could stand as sentences but that are *closely related,* especially

- when the second clause *expands* or explains the first:

  Neither of us spoke; we merely waited in silence to see what would happen.

- when the clauses describe a *sequence* of actions or *different aspects* of the same topic:

  There was a sharp, bracing air; the ground was dry; the sea was bright and clear.

- before independent clauses beginning with *even so, so, therefore, for instance, nevertheless, then,* etc.:

  He took great care; even so, he made a few errors.

- to suggest a contrast:

  I like swimming; my sister hates it.

In all the above examples periods could have been used but would have been too abrupt.

NOTE: The clause after the semicolon always begins with a small letter.

➤ to mark off a series of phrases or clauses that themselves contain commas:

  You will need the following: some scrap paper; a pen, preferably blue or black; some envelopes; and some good, white, unlined writing paper.

THE COLON IS USED

➤ to introduce a list (e.g., as in last entry on preceding page), long quotation, or speech:

> Speaking at Caesar's funeral, Antony addresses the crowd: "Friends, Romans, countrymen . . ."

It may also be used

➤ before a clause that explains (often by illustration) the previous statement. The colon has the force of the word *namely* or *that is:*

> One thing is certain: we shall not surrender.

Here a dash could have been used.

➤ to express a *strong* contrast:

> God creates: man destroys.

➤ to introduce a climax or concluding clause:

> After pondering the choices before him, he came to a decision: he joined the army.

➤ to make a pointed connection:

> Lenore became a director in just three months: her mother was the chief shareholder.

ELLIPSES (OR DOTS)

Three dots show the omission of one or more words within a passage, or a breaking off before the end of a sentence.

Four dots indicate an omission of one or more sentences after the end of a sentence, the first dot being the period.

PART II

WRITING ENGLISH

Chapter 5

Essays

Success in essay writing depends in large measure on how well you can adhere to the guidelines spelled out below. These do's and don'ts will help you write essays that are clear, interesting, and correct. Refer to them often. Over time, they will become second nature and guide you whenever you face a blank sheet of paper or an empty computer screen on which you must write an essay for school or any other occasion.

NARROW YOUR TOPIC

To avoid writing an essay filled with generalities about such broad topics as *democracy*, or *psychology*, or *jazz,* narrow the topic ruthlessly. The topic of a 250-word essay must be narrower than the topic of an essay of, say, 1,500 words. Try building a ladder of abstraction, starting at the top with the most general word. As you descend, make each rung increasingly specific. When you reach the bottom, you may have a topic suitable for a short essay. For example:

SUBJECT: Zoology

Zoology	Highest level of abstraction
The study of mammals	*Too broad for a short essay*
The study of primates	*Still very broad*
Researching the behavior of chimpanzees	*Still too broad*
Teaching chimps	*Still rather broad, but better*
Training chimps to distinguish colors	*A reasonable topic*
The job of an assistant working on the color recognition project in the primate lab	*A fine topic for a short paper*

WHAT TO INCLUDE

An essay needs a point, sometimes called a *main idea* or *thesis*. Don't confuse the topic of an essay with its point. A topic isn't enough. An essay must say something about its topic. For example, will you discuss an issue and take a position for or against it?

Assume for a moment that you are writing an essay about automobile seat belts. Your purpose may be to explain the use of seat belts or to describe how they function. Or maybe you intend to recount the history and development of seat belts, or to compare different types. Or you may wish to discuss state laws that require occupants of a car to buckle up. Although the purpose of the essay may be clear, an essay about seat belts must still make a point—perhaps that seat belt laws infringe on a driver's freedom of choice. Or its point might be that safety laws supercede a person's right to choose whether to wear seat belts. Or the essay may simply prove that driving without seat belts is dangerous and stupid.

Ordinarily, an essay should contain a sentence or two that spells out its thesis. Most often the thesis is stated early in the essay, but not always. Sometimes the thesis can appear at the very end. Or the thesis may be so strongly implied by the cumulative weight of evidence that stating it is unnecessary. In general, the content and organization of the essay will govern where you put the thesis or whether you state it at all.

COLLECT IDEAS

Once you have settled on a topic, jot down ideas freely for a few minutes, asking yourself questions on the subject. Then sort out the best material under paragraph headings and in a logical sequence. Let this serve as your outline, the plan to follow as you write.

The order of ideas is important. What should come first? Second? Third? The best order is the clearest order, the arrangement that readers can follow with the least effort. No plan is superior to another one provided you have a valid reason for using it. The plan least likely to succeed is the aimless one, the one in which you state and develop ideas in the random order they happened to come to mind. It's better to rank your ideas in the order of importance. Although your best argument may be listed first in your notes, save it for last on the essay. In other words, work toward your best point, not away from it.

An excellent way to plot three good ideas is to lead with the second best one, save the best for the end, and sandwich your least powerful idea between the others. This structure recognizes that the end and the beginning of the essay are its most critical parts.

OPENING AND CLOSING PARAGRAPHS

The opening lines of an essay tell the reader what to expect. If the opening is dull or confusing, readers will brace themselves for a less than thrilling reading experience. Begin with something that lures the reader into the essay. Use a "hook"—a phrase, sentence, or idea to grab your readers' interest.

Among many other techniques for essay openings, try any of these:

> Begin with a brief incident or anecdote that relates to the point of the essay.

> State a provocative idea in an ordinary way or an ordinary idea in a provocative way.

> Use a brief but memorable quotation related to the topic of your essay.

> Knock down a commonly held assumption or define a word in a new and startling way.

> Ask an interesting question or two that you will answer in the essay.

> Create suspense by withholding some information about a puzzling situation or dilemma.

When you reach the end of an essay, write a conclusion that leaves your reader a gift. What you leave can

Warnings

Remember that you are writing to a particular person.
Use his or her name or office/title.

THE LETTER

Layout

Although many formats exist for writing attractive and
effective business letters, you can't go wrong using the
layout described below. Leave a margin space of at
least $1\frac{1}{2}$ inches down the left-hand side and at top and
bottom, and 1 inch down the right-hand side.

5 Blank Street	(Your address)
Blankton, NJ 20117	
July 27, 1997	(Date in full)
Dean of Admissions	(Addressee)
State University	
Blankton, MI 48500	

Dear Sir or Madam:

....

....

Yours truly,

(Signature)

Notes on layout:

➤ In the sample addresses, the all-capitalized, unpunctu-
ated, two-letter Postal Service state abbreviation was
used. It is equally correct to spell out the state name.
But remember to be consistent; whatever form is used

for your return address should be used for the
addressee's address.

➤ Date in full, *not* 7-29-97 or July 29th.

➤ "Yours truly," on the left-hand side below the message.
Notice comma following.

➤ Beneath this, your signature *legibly* written. Beneath
this, your name typewritten.

Mode of Address and Closing

If you do not know the name of the addressee, use
"Dear Sir or Madam." If you do know the name of the
addressee, use "Dear Mr. Blank:" or "Dear Ms.
Blank:" A closing should be chosen that expresses the
appropriate degree of formality or informality (e.g.,
"Yours truly" would be formal; "Sincerely yours" less
formal; "Best regards," less formal still).

General

In general, aim at clarity, conciseness, and dignity of
expression. Be polite and direct. Avoid verbosity and
business jargon, as well as colloquialisms, slang, and
contractions.

If you are replying to a letter, you should normally
first thank the sender thus: "Thank you for your letter
of January 16."

Start a new paragraph for your message. It is
common now, particularly in business letters, not to
indent the first line of a paragraph. Instead, paragraphs
are separated by spaces between them. This is also
often done in books that consist of notes rather than
continuous text.

A **ballad** is a poem or folk song that tells a story, often in a dramatic form. The usual ballad has four-line stanzas with four stressed beats in the first and third lines and three in the second and fourth.

"Barbara Allen" and *The Rime of the Ancient Mariner*

Blank verse is unrhymed verse. Each line has ten syllables, the stress tending to fall on every second syllable. Such a meter is called iambic pentameter.

Was this the face that launched a thousand ships
And burnt the topless towers of Ilium?

A **conceit** is an ingeniously developed, often surprising, image or comparison. T. S. Eliot makes a witty and elaborate comparison between a London fog and a cat, and John Donne compares himself and his lover to the two arms of a pair of compasses.

A **couplet** is a pair of rhyming lines:

So long as men can breathe, or eyes can see,
So long lives this, and this gives life to thee.

Diction is the choice, use, and arrangement of words in a literary work.

An **elegy** is a formal poem of lament for the dead:

Gray's "Elegy Written in a Country Churchyard"

An **epic** is a long narrative poem or other work about heroic achievements. It is grand in style and scale.

Milton's *Paradise Lost,* Melville's *Moby Dick*

A **euphemism** is a mild or indirect way of describing an unpleasant or embarrassing thing:

> He passed away.

Foot/feet: the sound-unit, of two or three syllables, that is repeated in a line of verse. (See meter)

A **genre** is a form or type of literature:

> tragedy, comedy, epic poetry, science fiction, the short story

Hyperbole is exaggeration for effect:

> He ate mountains of pasta.

Imagery creates vivid pictures or sensations in the mind; it includes metaphors and similes. A poem may be an extended image or set of images.

> Out, out, brief candle.
> Life's but a walking shadow, a poor player
> That struts and frets his hour upon the stage
> And then is heard no more.

Here Macbeth, in a set of linked images, compares life to a candle, a shadow and an actor's brief spell upon the stage.

Irony

> **verbal**—when you mean the opposite of what the words state:

>> You're a nice one!

> Antony in *Julius Caesar* calls Caesar's assassins "honorable men" but means the opposite.

dramatic—When the audience or reader knows something that one or all of the characters on the stage don't know.

A **lyric** is words to a song or short poem expressing direct personal feeling:

Wordsworth's "I Wandered Lonely As a Cloud"

A **metaphor** is a condensed simile (without the words *like* or *as*). One thing is said to *be* the other thing with which it is compared.

The train *snaked* its way up the valley.
That boy is a *tiger.*

Meter is the rhythmic pattern and length of a line of verse. It consists of a number of metrical feet. The commonest of these are iambic, where an unstressed syllable is followed by a stressed one, e.g., ăgáin; and trochaic, where a stressed syllable is followed by an unstressed one, e.g., thōusănd.

A line with five feet is called a **pentameter:**

The curfew tolls the knell of parting day.

A line with four feet is called a **tetrameter:**

The ice was here; the ice was there.

An **ode** is a lyric poem in honor or praise of something. It is usually exalted in style and feeling.

Keats's "Ode on a Grecian Urn"

Onomatopoeia is using words which, through their own *sound,* imitate or suggest the sound of what they describe:

meow, buzz; the *blare* of trumpets; the *murmuring* of innumerable bees

A **paradox** is a saying that seems to contradict itself; its apparent nonsense, however, emphasizes a truth:

More haste, less speed.

A **persona** is a character and voice adopted by an author:

the Duke in Browning's "My Last Duchess"

Personification is treating an abstract quality as if it were human:

Justice holds the scales.
Fortune smiled on them.

It is also commonly used to endow nonhuman things with human feelings:

The kettle sang merrily.

"Pathetic fallacy" is ascribing human feelings to inanimate things.

the angry winds, the kind old sun

A **pun** is a play on words, either on two meanings of the same word, or on words sounding alike:

Drilling holes is *boring.*
Was King Kong the original urban *guerrilla*?

Satire is a work that holds vice or folly up to ridicule:

Gulliver's Travels is a satire on pride.

A **simile** brings out a point or points of likeness between two different things. It is usually introduced by the word *like* or *as:*

> Her skin was *as white as snow.*
> His hand was trembling *like a leaf*

A **soliloquy** is a speech in a play in which a character thinks aloud while alone on stage:

> Hamlet's "To be or not to be" speech

A **sonnet** is a fourteen-line poem usually in iambic pentameter with a rhyme scheme.

A **stanza** is a regular grouping of lines in a poem, used as a kind of verse paragraph.

A **symbol** is an object or set of objects standing for some idea:

> The *cross* is the symbol of Christianity.

The **theme** is the underlying idea, subject, or issue that the writer treats:

> *The Great Gatsby* treats the theme of the American Dream.

Tone is the writer's manner of speaking or attitude toward his or her subject and/or reader. This might be sarcastic, flippant, bitter, etc.

A **tragedy** is a play or other work that describes great suffering and catastrophe in a way that moves us to pity and horror:

> *King Lear*

Index

Notes

Notes

Notes